LET'S READ
ABOUT
Animals

Koalas

by Kathleen Pohl

Reading consultant: Susan Nations, M.Ed.,
author/literacy coach/consultant
in literacy development

Please visit our web site at: www.garethstevens.com
For a free color catalog describing Weekly Reader® Early Learning Library's list
of high-quality books, call 1-877-445-5824 (USA) or 1-800-387-3178 (Canada).
Weekly Reader® Early Learning Library's fax: (414) 336-0164.

Library of Congress Cataloging-in-Publication Data

Pohl, Kathleen.
  Koalas / by Kathleen Pohl.
    p. cm. — (Let's read about animals)
  Includes bibliographical references and index.
  ISBN-13: 978-0-8368-7818-9 (lib. bdg.)
  ISBN-13: 978-0-8368-7825-7 (softcover)
  1. Koalas—Juvenile literature. I. Title.
  QL737.M384P64 2007
  599.2—dc22   2006030868

This edition first published in 2007 by
Weekly Reader® Early Learning Library
A Member of the WRC Media Family of Companies
330 West Olive Street, Suite 100
Milwaukee, WI 53212 USA

Copyright © 2007 by Weekly Reader® Early Learning Library

Editor: Dorothy L. Gibbs
Art Direction: Tammy West
Cover design and page layout: Kami Strunsee
Picture research: Diane Laska-Swanke

Picture credits: Cover, title © John Shaw/Auscape; p. 5 © Pavel German/Auscape; p. 7 Kami Strunsee/
© Weekly Reader® Early Learning Library; pp. 9, 11, 17 © Jean-Paul Ferrero/Auscape; p. 13 © Steven David
Miller/Auscape; p. 15 © C. Andrew Henley/Auscape; p. 19 © D. Parer & E. Parer-Cook/Auscape; p. 21
© Klein/Hubert-Bios/Auscape

Printed in the United States of America

1 2 3 4 5 6 7 8 9 10 10 09 08 07 06

Note to Educators and Parents

Reading is such an exciting adventure for young children! They are beginning to integrate their oral language skills with written language. To encourage children along the path to early literacy, books must be colorful, engaging, and interesting; they should invite the young reader to explore both the print and the pictures.

The *Let's Read About Animals* series is designed to help children read and learn about the special characteristics and behaviors of the intriguing featured animals. Each book is an informative nonfiction companion to one of the colorful and charming fiction books in the *Animal Storybooks* series.

Each book in the *Let's Read About Animals* series is specially designed to support the young reader in the reading process. The familiar topics are appealing to young children and invite them to read — and reread — again and again. The full-color photographs and enhanced text further support the student during the reading process.

In addition to serving as wonderful picture books in schools, libraries, homes, and other places where children learn to love reading, these books are specifically intended to be read within an instructional guided reading group. This small group setting allows beginning readers to work with a fluent adult model as they make meaning from the text. After children develop fluency with the text and content, the books can be read independently. Children and adults alike will find these books supportive, engaging, and fun!

— Susan Nations, M.Ed., author/literacy coach/
consultant in literacy development

This animal looks like a teddy bear. It is not a bear at all! It is a **koala** (koh-AH-lah).

5

Koalas live in **Australia** (aw-STRAY-lee-ah). The map shows where koalas live in the wild.

Australia

Map Key

places koalas live

Koalas like to be in trees. They
eat and sleep in trees.

Koalas sleep a lot. They sleep up to twenty hours a day!

Their strong **claws** help koalas climb trees. They have to hang on tight!

claw

The toes on their paws are like fingers and thumbs. Koalas can curl their toes to grip objects.

toes

They use their front paws like hands to hold food. The only food a koala eats is **eucalyptus** (you-kuh-LIP-tus) **leaves**.

eucalyptus leaves

A newborn koala looks like a pink jelly bean. It grows inside its mother's **pouch** for six months. What other animal do you know that has a pouch?

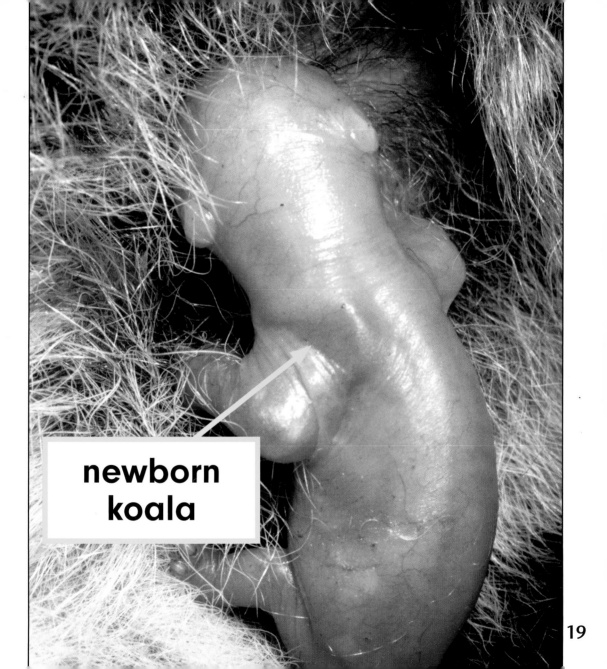

newborn
koala

19

A baby koala is called a **joey** (joh-ee). A big joey rides on its mother's back. Think of all it can see from up in that tree!

joey

Glossary

Australia — an island continent in the southern half of the world

eucalyptus leaves — the leaves of a special kind of tree in Australia that is often called a gum tree

grip — to hold by grasping tightly with curled fingers

joey — a baby animal that grows in its mother's pouch, such as a koala or a kangaroo

koala — a furry animal that looks like a bear and lives wild only in Australia

pouch — the special pocket that koalas and some other animals have on their bellies and use to hold their babies

For More Information

Books

Koala. Edana Eckart (Children's Press)

Koala. Busy Baby Animals (series). Jinny Johnson (Gareth Stevens)

Koala Commotion. Animal Storybooks (series). Rebecca Johnson (Gareth Stevens)

Koby the Koala. Wild Animal Families (series). Jan Latta (Gareth Stevens)

Web Site

Koalas for Kids

www.savethekoala.com/kids/indexkids.html

Look for facts, photos, and fun on this fascinating Web site from the Australian Koala Foundation. (The links are in a box on the far right side of the screen.)

Publisher's note to educators and parents: Our editors have carefully reviewed this Web site to ensure that it is suitable for children. Many Web sites change frequently, however, and we cannot guarantee that a site's future contents will continue to meet our high standards of quality and educational value. Be advised that children should be closely supervised whenever they access the Internet.

Index

About the Author

Kathleen Pohl has written and edited many children's books. Among them are animal tales, rhyming books, retold classics, and the forty-book series *Nature Close-Ups*. Most recently, she authored the Weekly Reader® Early Learning Library series *Where People Work*. She also served for many years as top editor of *Taste of Home* and *Country Woman* magazines. She and her husband, Bruce, live in the middle of beautiful Wisconsin woods and share their home with six goats, a llama, and all kinds of wonderful woodland creatures.